Granddaughter,
I Love You So Much

ISBN: 978-1-59842-983-1

Wonderful Wacky Women®
Inspiring•Uplifting•Empowering

is a trademark of Suzy and Al Toronto. Used under license.

and Blue Mountain Press are registered in U.S. Patent and Trademark Office. Certain trademarks are used under license.

Printed in China.
Eleventh Printing: 2021

⊕ This book is printed on recycled paper.

This book is printed on paper that has been specially produced to be acid free (neutral pH) and contains no groundwood or unbleached pulp. It conforms with the requirements of the American National Standards Institute, Inc., so as to ensure that this book will last and be enjoyed by future generations.

Blue Mountain Arts, Inc.
P.O. Box 4549, Boulder, Colorado 80306

Granddaughter,
I Love You So Much

Suzy Toronto

Blue Mountain Press™
Boulder, Colorado

To My Granddaughter... from My Heart to Yours

Few moments in my life
have been greater than
that very first time
I held you in my arms.
As you took a deep breath
and sighed one of your
sweet baby sighs, you took
my breath away. You were such a
great big miracle all packaged up
in the cutest, little,
teeny-tiny body,
and you just seemed
to smile all the time.

©Suzy Toronto

Holding you instantly put me in my
"happy place"... and became my very most favorite thing
to do in the history of forever! Your mom had
to practically pry you out of my arms.

As you grew, you became my favorite "hello"
and my hardest "goodbye." For in you,
I see eyes filled with adventure and dreams,
a mind spinning with unlimited possibilities
for the future, and a body filled with
unbound energy and enthusiasm.
You are my posterity... and my joy.

Folks often say that if they knew
grandchildren were so much fun,
they'd have had them first.
I agree... especially when it
comes to you.

Oh, my granddaughter!
I am so proud of you.

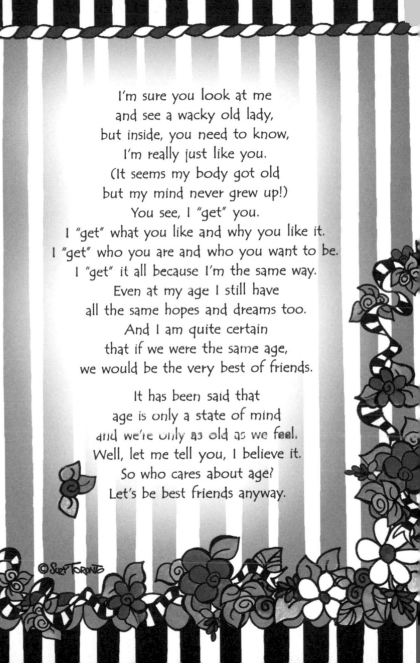

I'm sure you look at me
and see a wacky old lady,
but inside, you need to know,
I'm really just like you.
(It seems my body got old
but my mind never grew up!)
You see, I "get" you.
I "get" what you like and why you like it.
I "get" who you are and who you want to be.
I "get" it all because I'm the same way.
Even at my age I still have
all the same hopes and dreams too.
And I am quite certain
that if we were the same age,
we would be the very best of friends.

It has been said that
age is only a state of mind
and we're only as old as we feel.
Well, let me tell you, I believe it.
So who cares about age?
Let's be best friends anyway.

©Suzy Toronto

You Are Truly Wonderful!

I know you've heard me express
how special I think you are,
but what can I say?
It's part of being a grandparent.
Raving about our grandkids
is what we do best!

So here goes...

"You have everything it takes.
You're smart. You're enthusiastic.
And you're adorable inside and out!
You find fun and laughter in everything,
and you fearlessly tackle any challenge
that comes your way. But the thing
I admire most is that you balance
your outer beauty
with a heart and soul that are
kind, loving, and generous."

I could go on and on
about how great you are,
and I know that I'm not the only one
who feels this way!

©Suzy Toronto

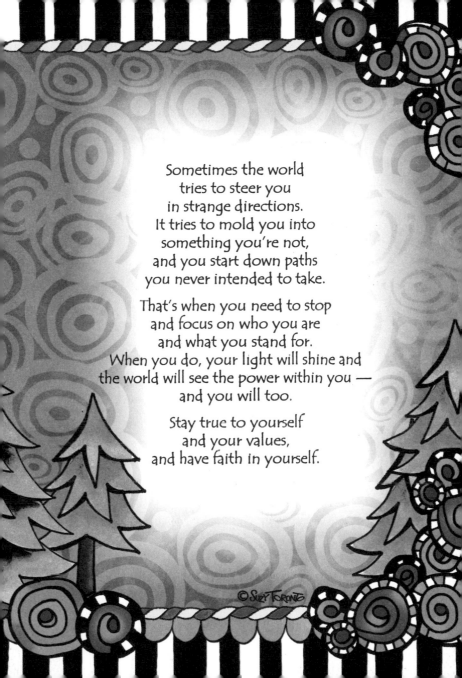

Sometimes the world
tries to steer you
in strange directions.
It tries to mold you into
something you're not,
and you start down paths
you never intended to take.

That's when you need to stop
and focus on who you are
and what you stand for.
When you do, your light will shine and
the world will see the power within you —
and you will too.

Stay true to yourself
and your values,
and have faith in yourself.

© Suzy Toronto

Embrace both the triumphs
and the tragedies of life
as the rich growth opportunities they are,
and refuse to let either one
distort your view.

See new possibilities at every juncture.
Make the world a better place
and infinitely more interesting.

With wild abandon,
seize the moment
and truly live every minute of your life.
Bask in unparalleled opportunities
for the chance to be more.
Evolve into the magnificent creature
God always intended you to be.

Wonderful Wacky Words of Wisdom
I Hope You Will Always Remember

You are capable of more than you have ever imagined 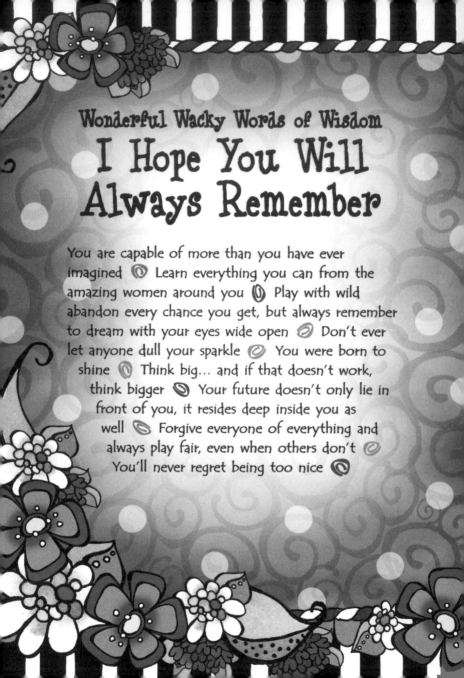 Learn everything you can from the amazing women around you Play with wild abandon every chance you get, but always remember to dream with your eyes wide open Don't ever let anyone dull your sparkle You were born to shine Think big... and if that doesn't work, think bigger Your future doesn't only lie in front of you, it resides deep inside you as well Forgive everyone of everything and always play fair, even when others don't You'll never regret being too nice

Honor your legacy with your integrity
Remember, there's no right way to do a
wrong thing Be happy and know that
no one can make you feel inferior unless
you give them permission
to do so And
in the end, good
girls always
win

© Suzy Toronto

Anyone who says
she doesn't need a girlfriend
just hasn't found a good one yet.

With a girlfriend,
you just can't bear the thought
of picking up the phone
and not having her
on the other end
to talk to, cry to, and visit with.
She's your biggest critic,
head cheerleader,
and favorite sounding board
all rolled into one.

Your life is infinitely more interesting,
fun, exciting, peaceful, joyous, and real
simply because she's in it.

You're blessed if you have
a girlfriend like this.

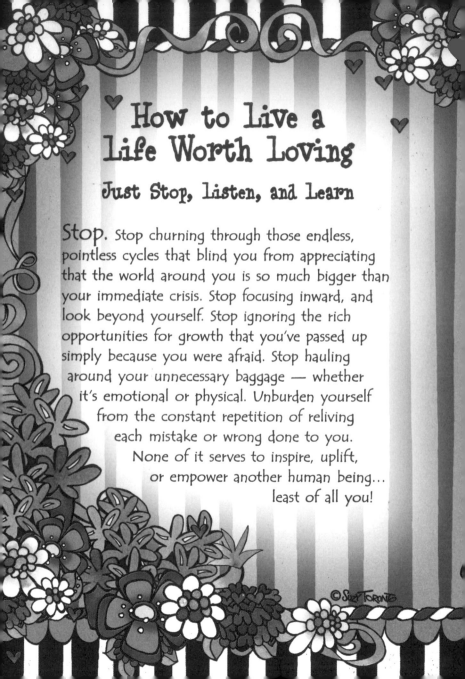

How to Live a Life Worth Loving

Just Stop, Listen, and Learn

Stop. Stop churning through those endless, pointless cycles that blind you from appreciating that the world around you is so much bigger than your immediate crisis. Stop focusing inward, and look beyond yourself. Stop ignoring the rich opportunities for growth that you've passed up simply because you were afraid. Stop hauling around your unnecessary baggage — whether it's emotional or physical. Unburden yourself from the constant repetition of reliving each mistake or wrong done to you. None of it serves to inspire, uplift, or empower another human being... least of all you!

♥ **Listen.** Listen to your breathing, to your heartbeat. Listen to the sound of the ocean, the rustle of leaves in the wind, and the silence of softly falling snow. Stop talking... and really take the time to just listen.

Seek out those who have accomplished astonishing feats, and listen to what they have to say. Absorb all that is good in them, and let the rest drift away. Drink in the wisdom they have to offer. Such wisdom is everywhere, if you will just open your heart and listen...

Learn. Learn from your parents. Learn from your teachers. Learn from those who love you — and, even more, from those who don't. Admit that you are not always right and that you don't have all the answers.

Try to look at every situation from another perspective. Learn to take a chance and make a change. Accept obstacles and challenges as opportunities to grow and become a better person. These are among our greatest gifts, but we must have the grace to accept them.

© Suz Toronto

Here's the real irony of life:
in order for growth to be all about you,
you have to stop thinking about yourself,
listen to the wisdom of those around you,
and learn from it all.

So you see,
it's really quite easy...
Just stop, listen,
and learn.

Wonderful Wacky Words...
Live Your Life with Passion and Purpose

When you do something goofy, do it with enthusiasm ◎ There's no such thing as "can't"... you CAN do it ◐ Don't wait to live your dreams — jump in with both feet and go for it ◉ Wacky spontaneity and enthusiasm trump technique and expertise every time ◐

Dare to be remarkable 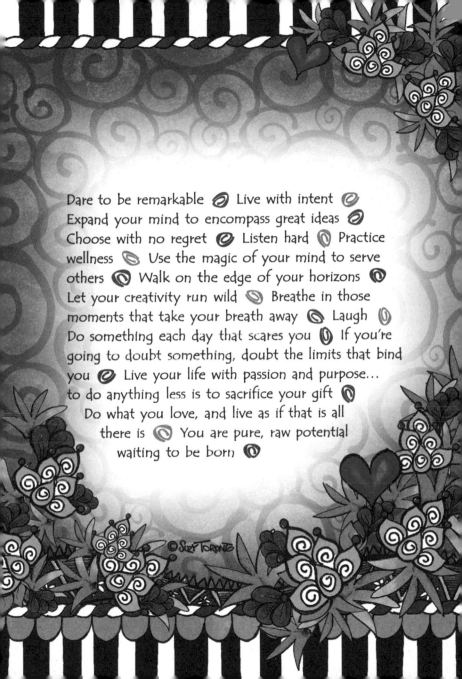 Live with intent
Expand your mind to encompass great ideas
Choose with no regret Listen hard Practice
wellness Use the magic of your mind to serve
others Walk on the edge of your horizons
Let your creativity run wild Breathe in those
moments that take your breath away Laugh
Do something each day that scares you If you're
going to doubt something, doubt the limits that bind
you Live your life with passion and purpose...
to do anything less is to sacrifice your gift
Do what you love, and live as if that is all
there is You are pure, raw potential
waiting to be born

© Suzy Toronto

Some Days You Just Have to Act "As If"

...you know, "as if" *everything* is okay, "as if" everything is **normal**, and "as if" *everything* is just business as usual (despite the fact that you **Know** it's just an act, and the reality of it all seems *completely* overwhelming!). But sometimes you just have to put on your *game face* and press forward with **faith**.

You have to **reach** down into
yourself deeper than you ever have to
find **strength** and *courage*,
even when your own doubt and fear
try to convince you to give up.

But what if just around the next corner
a **shiny** brass ring is *waiting for you?*
What if the **rainbow's end** is just around
the bend? What if you hang in there for just
one more **minute?** **Miracles** just might
happen. This is **not** the time to wimp out
and be a **chicken.** This is the time
to **stand up** straight, throw your
shoulders back, and act "as if"
nothing were **Impossible.**
You can do it. I know you can!
All you have to do is
fake it 'til you make it!
(Grandma said so!)

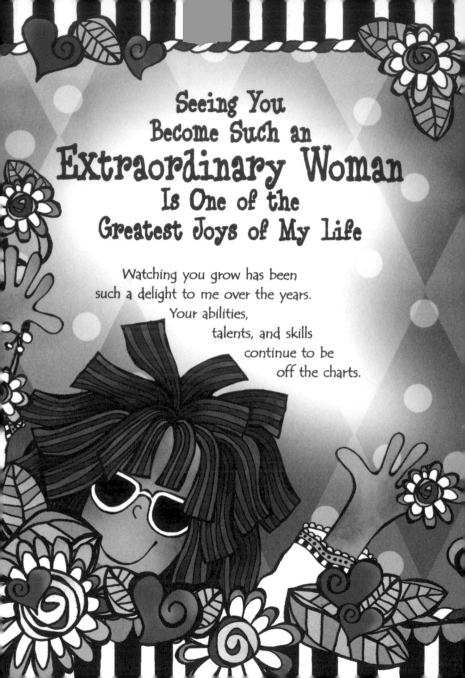

Seeing You
Become Such an
Extraordinary Woman
Is One of the
Greatest Joys of My Life

Watching you grow has been
such a delight to me over the years.
Your abilities,
talents, and skills
continue to be
off the charts.

It is so fun to watch
as you find your place in the world
with such strength and character.
With each step you have taken,
every achievement you have conquered,
and every dream you "go for,"
all my hopes and dreams go with you.

It has been such a joy for me
to travel alongside you
and to witness the glorious
promise of your future.
There is simply no counting
the blessings you have been to me
or any way to measure the joy
you have brought to my life.
I just want you to know that
I love you more than any words can say,
any hug can show,
or any feelings can express.

Forever, for always, and no matter what.

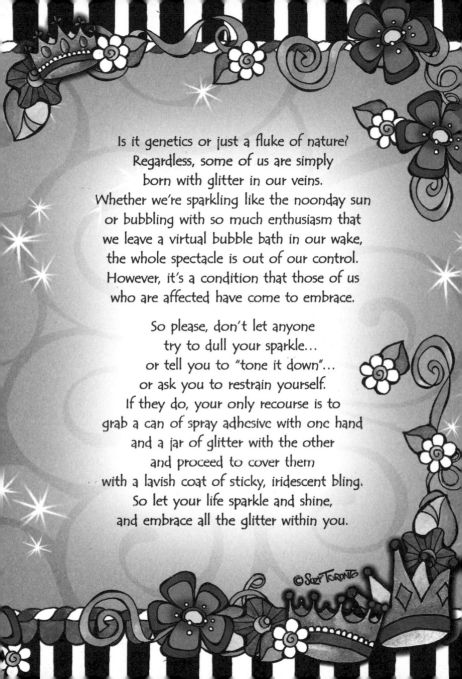

Is it genetics or just a fluke of nature?
Regardless, some of us are simply
born with glitter in our veins.
Whether we're sparkling like the noonday sun
or bubbling with so much enthusiasm that
we leave a virtual bubble bath in our wake,
the whole spectacle is out of our control.
However, it's a condition that those of us
who are affected have come to embrace.

So please, don't let anyone
try to dull your sparkle...
or tell you to "tone it down"...
or ask you to restrain yourself.
If they do, your only recourse is to
grab a can of spray adhesive with one hand
and a jar of glitter with the other
and proceed to cover them
with a lavish coat of sticky, iridescent bling.
So let your life sparkle and shine,
and embrace all the glitter within you.

© Suzy Toronto

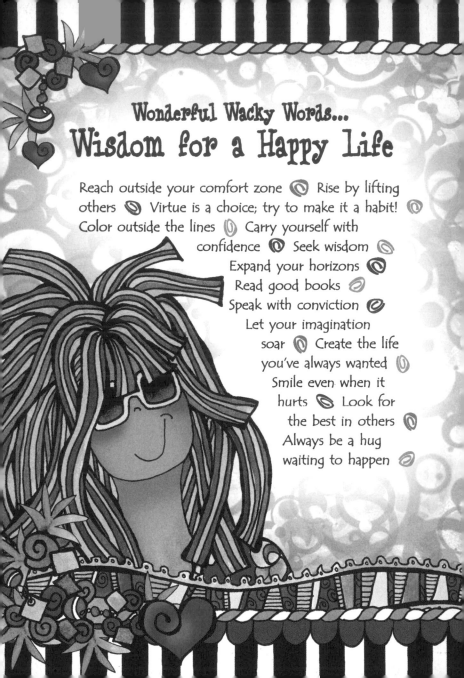

Wonderful Wacky Words...
Wisdom for a Happy Life

Reach outside your comfort zone ◎ Rise by lifting
others ◎ Virtue is a choice; try to make it a habit! ◎
Color outside the lines ◎ Carry yourself with
confidence ◎ Seek wisdom ◎
Expand your horizons ◎
Read good books ◎
Speak with conviction ◎
Let your imagination
soar ◎ Create the life
you've always wanted ◎
Smile even when it
hurts ◎ Look for
the best in others ◎
Always be a hug
waiting to happen ◎

Choose the right thing... even when it's not the easiest choice 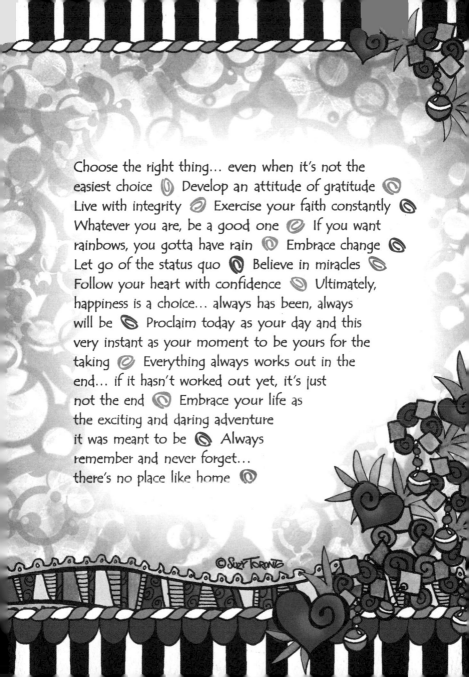 Develop an attitude of gratitude Live with integrity Exercise your faith constantly Whatever you are, be a good one If you want rainbows, you gotta have rain Embrace change Let go of the status quo Believe in miracles Follow your heart with confidence Ultimately, happiness is a choice... always has been, always will be Proclaim today as your day and this very instant as your moment to be yours for the taking Everything always works out in the end... if it hasn't worked out yet, it's just not the end Embrace your life as the exciting and daring adventure it was meant to be Always remember and never forget... there's no place like home

©Suzy Toronto

My Sweet Granddaughter,
You Bring Me Such Joy!

When I think about
how rich and full my life is,
I immediately think of you.

You have brought me
so much joy over the years.
Some of my fondest memories
center on the time
I have spent with you.

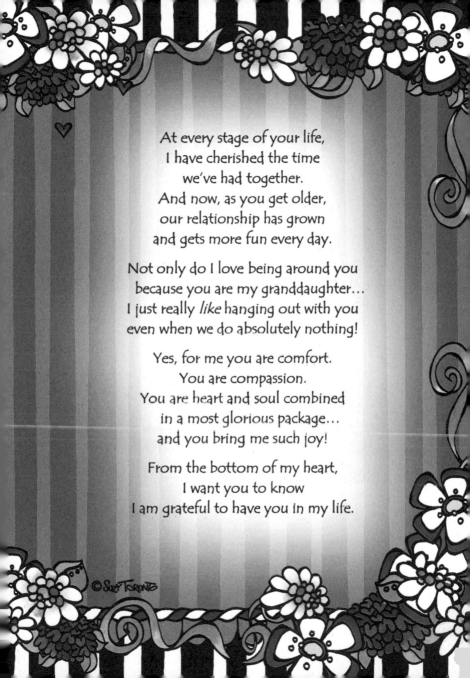

At every stage of your life,
I have cherished the time
we've had together.
And now, as you get older,
our relationship has grown
and gets more fun every day.

Not only do I love being around you
because you are my granddaughter...
I just really *like* hanging out with you
even when we do absolutely nothing!

Yes, for me you are comfort.
You are compassion.
You are heart and soul combined
in a most glorious package...
and you bring me such joy!

From the bottom of my heart,
I want you to know
I am grateful to have you in my life.

You're So Much More Than
My Granddaughter

The first time
I held you
in my arms,
I never wanted to
let you go.
And I knew at
that very moment
my heart would be
intertwined with
yours forever.

©Suzy Toronto

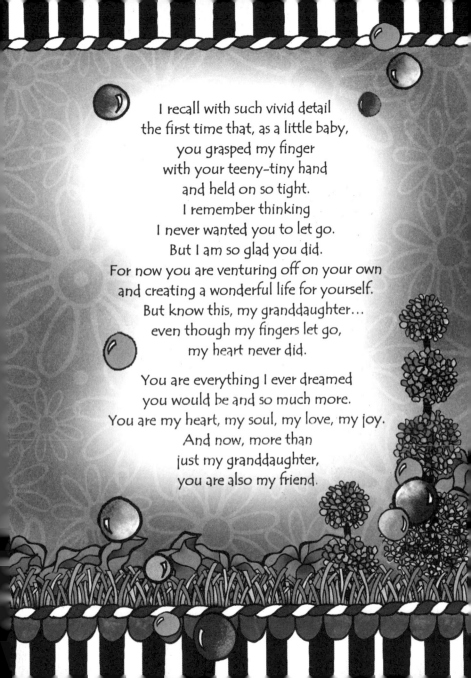

I recall with such vivid detail
the first time that, as a little baby,
you grasped my finger
with your teeny-tiny hand
and held on so tight.
I remember thinking
I never wanted you to let go.
But I am so glad you did.
For now you are venturing off on your own
and creating a wonderful life for yourself.
But know this, my granddaughter…
even though my fingers let go,
my heart never did.

You are everything I ever dreamed
you would be and so much more.
You are my heart, my soul, my love, my joy.
And now, more than
just my granddaughter,
you are also my friend.

If I could be there right now,
I'd wrap both my arms around you so tight
and never let you go.
I'd be like one of those "long huggers"
who hug way past
the point of your comfort zone.

I'd hug you until you felt
all the wonderful, warm, and
fuzzy feelings I have for you.
Then I'd start telling you
how totally amazing you are.
I'd ramble on and on about
all the greatness and courage I see in you.
I'm sure you'd roll your eyes and gasp for air,
but I wouldn't let that stop me.

It's not that my hug and
ramblings would solve anything,
but they would sure make me feel better.

I love you a bunch…
just want you to know.

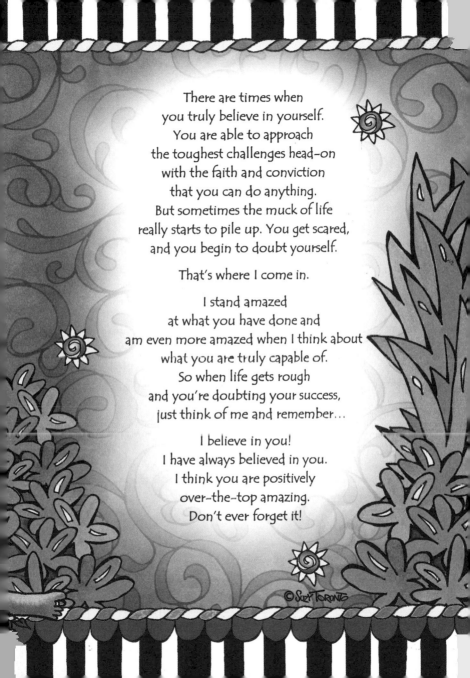

There are times when
you truly believe in yourself.
You are able to approach
the toughest challenges head-on
with the faith and conviction
that you can do anything.
But sometimes the muck of life
really starts to pile up. You get scared,
and you begin to doubt yourself.

That's where I come in.

I stand amazed
at what you have done and
am even more amazed when I think about
what you are truly capable of.
So when life gets rough
and you're doubting your success,
just think of me and remember…

I believe in you!
I have always believed in you.
I think you are positively
over-the-top amazing.
Don't ever forget it!

© Suzy Toronto

About the Author

So this is me… I'm a tad wacky and just shy of crazy. I'm fiftysomething and live in the sleepy village of Tangerine, Florida, with my husband, Al, and a big, goofy dog named Lucy. And because life wasn't crazy enough, my eightysomething-year-old parents live with us too. (In my home, the nuts don't fall far from the tree!) I eat far too much chocolate, and I drink sparkling water by the gallon. I practice yoga, ride a little red scooter, and go to the beach every chance I get. I have five grown children and over a dozen grandkids who love me as much as I adore them. I teach them to dip their French fries in their chocolate shakes and to make up any old words to the tunes they like. But most of all, I teach them to never, ever color inside the lines. This is the Wild Wacky Wonderful life I lead, and I wouldn't have it any other way. Welcome to my world!